Legacy

Secured

Protect Your Finances, Family, and Future

Copyright

This book was a labor of love, with every detail: writing,
cover design, editing, and layout.
by Aaron B. Kershaw.

Language: English

Publication Date: January 2025

Format: eBook, Paperback
ISBN: 979-8-90345-008-4
2nd Edition
BuildingBlocs Publishing, Inc

Cover: Dall-E Photo
Cover Design: Aaron B. Kershaw

Copyright © 2025 Aaron B. Kershaw

For permission requests, contact the publisher at:

BuildingBlocs Publishing, Inc

www.BuildingBlocs.org

akershaw@buildingblocs.org

Legacy Secured: Protect Your Finances, Family, and Future

Published in the United States of America

Table of Contents

Securing Your Legacy

"It's Never Too Late to Secure Your Future & Protect Your Family"

Let me take you back to 2016, a year that changed everything for me. Up until that point, I'd been earning a good living, keeping things afloat, and thinking I had it all under control. And then, in what felt like the blink of an eye, I lost my ability to work. Just like that, my income dried up. I didn't see it coming, and I definitely wasn't ready for it.

The next few years weren't easy. Bills piled up. Savings dwindled. And I had to face the hard truth: I didn't know what I didn't know. Sure, I'd always thought I was doing "okay" financially, but when push came to shove, I realized I wasn't as prepared as I thought.

But here's the thing about hitting rock bottom, it teaches you a lot, fast. I went back to school, earned my financial licenses, and became an insurance professional. I started learning everything I could about how to navigate the financial maze of retirement, how to protect a family's legacy, and how to make sense of all the things no one ever really explains to you, like how Medicare sounds great on paper but comes with gaps you need to plan for, or how putting your house in a simple will might not protect it the way you think it will.

I realized that most people aren't struggling because they've made bad choices, they're struggling because no one ever taught them how the system works. And that's why I'm here. I've been through the struggles, the sleepless nights, and the uncertainty. And now, I'm here to share what I've learned, so you don't have to go through the same thing.

Why This Book Matters

Let's be honest: thinking about your finances, your retirement, and your legacy probably doesn't feel like a fun way to spend your time. But here's the truth: if you don't take the time to plan now, it could cost your family later.

Imagine this: you've worked hard your whole life, built up a nest egg, and paid off your home. You're thinking, *"I've done my part, my family is set."* But what if I told you that without the right planning, everything you've worked for could be at risk? A medical emergency, an unexpected lawsuit, or even simple misunderstandings about how inheritance laws work could jeopardize your legacy.

Here's another truth: the system isn't set up to make this easy for you. Medicare, Medicaid, life insurance, trusts, wills, they all sound great, but unless you understand the fine print, you could be leaving your family with a mess to clean up.

This book is about changing that. It's about giving you the tools, knowledge, and confidence to take control of your financial future. Because whether you're navigating Social Security, figuring out long-term care options, or deciding how to protect your home for your grandchildren, there's a lot to know, and a lot at stake.

What This Book Will Help You Do

This isn't just another financial book. It's a roadmap, written in plain English, from someone who's been there. Here's what we're going to tackle together:

1. **Making Your Money Work for You**: We'll start with the basics, budgeting on a fixed income, managing rising costs, and ensuring your money lasts as long as you do.

2. **Protecting What You've Built**: From understanding Medicare's gaps to navigating property insurance and long-term care, we'll cover the strategies that keep your assets safe.

3. **Leaving a Legacy You're Proud Of**: Whether it's creating a will, setting up a trust, or talking to your family about end-of-life wishes, we'll ensure you're leaving behind more than just money, you're leaving security, clarity, and love.

A Word of Reassurance

Now, I know this stuff can feel overwhelming. I've had those moments, sitting at the kitchen table with a stack of bills and insurance policies, thinking, *"Where do I even start?"* But here's the good news: you don't have to figure it all out at once. This book is designed to guide you step by step, breaking everything down into manageable pieces.

It's never too late to take control of your financial future, whether you're just starting to think about it or you've already got a plan in place. No matter where you're starting from, I'm here to help you make sense of it all and give you the peace of mind that comes with knowing you've got things handled.

What You'll Learn in This Book

This book is divided into three parts, each one building on the last:

Part 1: Financial Mastery in Retirement

We'll start with the foundation, how to budget, save, and stretch your income so you can enjoy retirement without constantly worrying about money.

Part 2: Building Security and Peace of Mind

Next, we'll focus on protecting what you've built. From healthcare costs to property insurance to long-term care planning, we'll tackle the big questions that can keep you up at night.

Part 3: Creating and Celebrating Your Legacy

Finally, we'll dive into legacy planning, ensuring your family is taken care of and your wishes are honored. We'll cover wills, trusts, family conversations, and even ways to give back to your community.

Why You Should Start Now

Here's the bottom line: your legacy is too important to leave to chance. You've worked hard to build a life for yourself and your family, and you deserve the peace of mind that comes with knowing it's protected.

So, let's get started. Let's take the first step toward securing your finances, protecting your family, and creating a legacy that reflects the values you hold dear.

Because when the time comes, your family shouldn't be left guessing, they should know that you've planned for them, loved them, and given them the gift of security.

"Your future isn't just about numbers. It's about peace of mind, clarity, and the legacy you'll leave behind. Let's make it one to be proud of."
– Uncle Aaron

Chapter One

Making Every Dollar Count

"Stretch Your Dollars, Live Your Dreams"

Let me tell you about Rick. Rick is a retired firefighter, a Vietnam veteran with a 70% VA disability rating, and one of the most dedicated dads I know. Between his fire department pension, VA disability payments, and Social Security benefits, Rick brings in about $6,500 a month, not bad, right? But as Rick would tell you, it's not as simple as it sounds.

Rick's divorced, and like many parents, he's still helping his kids with college tuition. Add in the rising costs of groceries, gas, and healthcare, and it's easy to see how his monthly income can feel stretched thin. "Aaron," he told me, "I thought I had this figured out, but now I'm not so sure. I've been reading *Budget Like a Boss,* and it's opened my eyes to how much I've been winging it."

Rick's story isn't unique. Plenty of retirees have multiple income streams but still feel like their money doesn't go as far as it should. But here's the good news: Rick's already taken the most important step, he's willing to learn. And with a little planning, we can make sure he's not just surviving in retirement but thriving.

Why a Budget is Essential in Retirement

Here's the thing about budgeting: it's not just for people who are struggling. Even if you have a solid income, like Rick does, a budget ensures your money reflects your priorities. Without one, it's too easy for your spending to get away from you, and before you know it, you're wondering where it all went.

For retirees, budgeting is even more important because your income is often fixed. That means you don't have the luxury of "just working overtime" or picking up a second job to cover unexpected costs. A budget puts you in control, making sure every dollar has a job and nothing goes to waste.

The 50/30/20 Rule for Seniors

One of the key principles in *Budget Like a Boss* is the 50/30/20 rule, and it works just as well for retirees as it does for younger folks. The idea is simple: divide your income into three categories, needs, wants, and savings.

Here's how we applied it to Rick's situation:

1. **50% Needs**: Housing, utilities, groceries, healthcare, and insurance.

2. **30% Wants**: Hobbies, dining out, travel, and family expenses (like helping the kids with college).

3. **20% Savings and Emergencies**: Building a cushion for unexpected expenses or longer-term goals.

Rick's Budget Breakdown

Rick's $6,500 monthly income was divided like this:

- **50% Needs:** $3,250 for rent, utilities, groceries, healthcare, and insurance.

- **30% Wants:** $1,950 for hobbies, dining out, and helping his kids with tuition.

- **20% Savings:** $1,300 for building an emergency fund and setting aside money for his next vacation.

When we first sat down, Rick admitted he'd been spending closer to 40% on "wants" without even realizing it. By reallocating his budget, he freed up an extra $300 a month to put toward savings and family goals.

Step 1: Tracking Spending, The Eye-Opener

Before we could fix Rick's budget, we had to figure out where his money was going. That's where tracking comes in.

Rick's "Aha" Moment

In *Budget Like a Boss,* I stress the importance of tracking every dollar for at least one month. Rick decided to give it a try, using a notebook to jot down all his expenses. At the end of the month, here's what he found:

- $600 a month on dining out.

- $150 on streaming services, apps, and subscriptions.

- $200 in "miscellaneous" purchases, things like coffee runs, snacks, and impulse buys.

"That's over $900 a month I didn't even realize I was spending," Rick told me. "No wonder it felt like I was always running out of money."

How to Track Your Spending

- **Low-Tech Option:** Use a notebook or printout to record every purchase.

- **High-Tech Option:** Apps like Mint or Goodbudget automatically categorize your expenses.

- **Weekly Review:** Spend 10 minutes each Sunday reviewing where your money went.

Step 2: Cutting Costs Without Sacrificing Joy

A budget shouldn't feel like a punishment. It's about cutting out what doesn't serve you so you can spend on what does.

1. Trimming the Fat

Rick found some easy places to cut:

- He canceled two streaming services he never used, saving $25 a month.

- He called his cell phone provider and negotiated a $40 discount.

- He started meal prepping to cut his dining-out budget in half, saving $300 a month.

2. Dining Out on a Budget

Rick and I came up with a plan:

- Cook at home during the week and reserve dining out for weekends.

- Use coupons and senior discounts when eating out.

These changes didn't feel restrictive, they freed up money for things Rick actually valued, like traveling and helping his kids with tuition.

3. Leveraging Senior Discounts

Rick hadn't realized just how many discounts were available to him as a veteran and a retiree. AARP memberships, veteran discounts, and local programs added up to savings on everything from groceries to travel.

Step 3: Building an Emergency Fund

Even in retirement, an emergency fund is critical. Life happens, cars break down, roofs need repairs, or medical bills pop up. Without a cushion, those expenses can derail your entire budget.

Start Small, Think Big

Rick started by saving $50 a month. "It didn't feel like much at first," he admitted, "but after a year, I had $600 in the bank, and that felt amazing."

Where to Keep Your Emergency Fund

- **High-Yield Savings Account**: Earns more interest than a traditional account.

- **Money Market Account**: A safe, low-risk place to grow your savings.

VA Benefits, Social Security, and Maximizing Income

Rick's VA benefits and Social Security were key parts of his financial picture. Here's how we made the most of them:

1. VA Disability Payments

Rick's 70% VA rating brought in $1,700 a month, tax-free. We allocated this income toward predictable expenses, like groceries and utilities, which gave him more flexibility with his pension and Social Security.

2. Social Security

Rick's $1,800 in Social Security payments helped cover tuition contributions for his kids. We also talked about coordinating withdrawals from his pension and Social Security to minimize taxes.

3. Exploring VA Education Benefits

I reminded Rick about VA programs like the Dependents' Educational Assistance (DEA), which could help his kids with tuition. Programs like this are often overlooked but can make a big difference.

Tools to Simplify Budgeting

Rick started using apps and tools to make budgeting easier:

- **Mint:** Tracked his spending and categorized expenses automatically.

- **Goodbudget:** Helped him set limits for dining out and hobbies.

- **Google Sheets:** Rick used a custom spreadsheet to track his budget and long-term goals.

The Emotional Side of Money

Money isn't just about numbers, it's emotional. It's tied to our sense of security, freedom, and even self-worth. Rick admitted that before he started budgeting, he felt stressed and ashamed about not having better control. But as he made changes, his confidence grew.

"Man, it feels good to know where my money's going," he told me. "I'm finally in control instead of feeling like my money's controlling me."

Rick's Breakthrough Moment

Six months after implementing his budget, Rick's finances looked completely different. He had a small but growing emergency fund, predictable tuition contributions, and enough left over to plan a trip to visit his daughter.

"You know what, Aaron? For the first time in a long time, I feel like I'm actually enjoying my retirement," he said.

Action Plan for the Week

Here's your homework for the week:

1. **Track Your Spending**: Write down every dollar you spend for seven days.

2. **Build Your Budget**: Use the 50/30/20 rule to create a basic budget.

3. **Find One Cut**: Look for one expense to reduce or eliminate and put that money into savings or something you love.

Every Dollar Has a Purpose

Your money is a tool, and budgeting helps you use it wisely. Whether you're saving for a big goal, covering everyday costs, or just trying to sleep better at night, the key is to make every dollar work for you.

Start small. Stay consistent. And remember you're not alone in this. With a little planning, you can stretch your dollars, live your dreams, and enjoy the retirement you deserve.

"A budget isn't about saying no, it's about saying yes to the things that matter most."

Chapter Two

Smart Spending, Smart Saving

"Protect What You've Earned, Save for What You Need"

Let me tell you about my cousin Laura. She's one of the smartest people I know, ran her own small business for years, raised three kids, and always seemed to have it together. But a few years back, she gave me a call that I wasn't expecting. "Aaron," she said, "I think I messed up. I got a call from someone claiming to be from my bank, and now I'm missing $2,500."

I could hear the embarrassment in her voice. She's no fool, but this scammer had been convincing. They had all the right details, her name, her account information, even a "case number" for supposed fraud. Laura had panicked and given them access to her account before realizing something didn't feel right.

She wasn't just upset about the money, she was mad at herself for falling for it. But here's the thing: these scams are designed to prey on good people, especially older adults who may not be as familiar with digital technology or the sneaky tactics scammers use.

Laura's story didn't end there, though. After the initial shock, we worked together to secure her finances, build an emergency fund, and make sure she was never caught off guard again. Her experience taught me something important: protecting what you've earned isn't just about making smart spending choices, it's about being proactive, staying alert, and having a plan for the unexpected.

Why Smart Spending and Saving Matter

If you're reading this book, chances are you've spent decades working hard, saving where you could, and building a life for yourself and your family. But even in retirement, smart spending and saving remain essential. Why? Because life doesn't stop throwing curveballs just because you're no longer working.

The good news is that it's never too late to start. Whether you're looking to build a safety net, protect yourself from scams, or stretch your dollars further, there's always a way to take control of your finances, no matter where you're starting from.

Building an Emergency Fund

"Start Small, Think Big"

Let's start with the foundation of any good financial plan: the emergency fund. If you're like most people, you've probably thought, *"I'll save for emergencies someday when I have extra money."* But here's the thing, there's never going to be a perfect time to start saving.

You have to start where you are, even if it's just a little at a time.

1. Why an Emergency Fund is Essential

Emergencies come in all shapes and sizes: a car repair, a broken water heater, an unexpected medical bill. Without a cushion, these expenses can wreak havoc on your budget and leave you scrambling.

2. How Much Should You Save?

The rule of thumb is to aim for three to six months' worth of expenses, but don't let that number intimidate you. The goal isn't perfection, it's progress. Even a small emergency fund can make a big difference.

3. Start Small and Stay Consistent

Laura started by saving just $20 a week. "It didn't feel like much at first," she said, "but after a few months, I looked at my account and realized I had $400. That felt amazing."

Where to Keep Your Emergency Fund

- **High-Yield Savings Account:** These accounts earn more interest than traditional savings accounts.

- **Money Market Account:** Another safe, low-risk option.

Avoiding Scams: Protecting What You've Earned

"If It Feels Wrong, Trust Your Gut"

Scams are everywhere these days, and seniors are often prime targets. Scammers know how to exploit trust, fear, and even kindness to trick you into handing over your hard-earned money.

1. Common Scams Targeting Seniors

Here are some of the most common scams to watch out for:

- **Phishing Emails and Calls:** Scammers pretend to be from your bank, the IRS, or Medicare and ask for personal information.

- **Fake Charities:** These pop up after natural disasters or around the holidays, tugging at your heartstrings.

- **Tech Support Scams:** Someone calls claiming your computer has a virus and asks for remote access or payment for "repairs."

- **Grandparent Scams:** A scammer pretends to be your grandchild in trouble, asking for money urgently.

2. Red Flags to Watch For

- They ask for payment in gift cards, wire transfers, or cryptocurrency.

- They create a sense of urgency, saying things like, "Act now, or you'll lose access to your account."

- They refuse to provide proof of who they are.

- The email or phone number looks suspicious (e.g., a Gmail address claiming to be from your bank).

3. How to Protect Yourself

- **Pause Before Acting:** Scammers thrive on panic. Take a moment to think before responding.

- **Verify the Source:** If someone claims to be from your bank, hang up and call the official number on the back of your debit card.

- **Set Up Alerts:** Many banks allow you to set up text or email alerts for suspicious activity.

- **Never Share Personal Info Over the Phone:** Legitimate organizations will never ask for your Social Security number, bank account details, or passwords over the phone.

Late-Life Saving Strategies

"Every Little Bit Counts"

Even if you're retired and on a fixed income, it's still possible to save money. The key is to find small, manageable ways to cut costs and redirect those savings into your emergency fund or future goals.

1. Downsizing Subscriptions

Take a look at your monthly subscriptions. Are you paying for streaming services you rarely use? What about magazines, meal kits, or gym memberships? Canceling just one or two unused subscriptions could save you $20–$50 a month.

2. Finding Senior Discounts

There are discounts out there for everything from dining to travel to insurance. Here are a few examples:

- **Restaurants:** Many offer 10%–20% off for seniors, just ask.
- **Travel:** Airlines, hotels, and car rental companies often have special rates for older adults.
- **Retail Stores:** Chains like Kohl's and Ross offer senior discount days.

3. Embracing DIY

Instead of hiring someone for small tasks, consider doing them yourself. Whether it's minor home repairs, gardening, or even cooking more meals at home, DIY saves money while keeping you active.

4. Set Goals for Your Savings

When you have a clear goal, it's easier to stay motivated. For Laura, it was building up her emergency fund to $1,000. For you, it might be saving for a vacation, a new appliance, or simply having peace of mind.

Activity: Spotting Scams and Starting Your Fund

Here's an actionable plan for this week:

1. **Scam Checklist:**

   - Did the person contact you unexpectedly?

   - Are they asking for personal or financial information?

   - Are they pressuring you to act immediately?

   - Are they asking for payment in unusual forms (like gift cards)?

If the answer to any of these questions is "yes," it's probably a scam.

2. **Emergency Fund Steps:**

   - Decide how much you can save each week, start with as little as $10.

   - Open a high-yield savings account if you don't already have one.

   - Automate your savings to make it consistent.

The Emotional Side of Saving

Money isn't just numbers on a page, it's tied to how we feel about security, freedom, and the future. For Laura, rebuilding her confidence after the scam was just as important as rebuilding her emergency fund. "Knowing I'm prepared for the unexpected gives me peace of mind," she told me. "It's like a weight has been lifted."

Laura's Breakthrough Moment

Six months after starting her emergency fund, Laura had saved $750. She'd also installed scam alerts on her bank accounts and educated her friends about how to spot phishing emails. "I feel like I've taken my power back," she said. And that's what this chapter is all about: empowering yourself to protect what you've earned and save for what you need.

Action Plan for the Week

Here's your to-do list for this week:

1. **Set Your Savings Goal:** Decide how much you want to save for emergencies.

2. **Track Your Subscriptions:** Look for one or two subscriptions you can cancel or downgrade.

3. **Educate Yourself on Scams:** Share the scam checklist with a friend or family member.

Protect and Prepare

Protecting your money and saving for the future isn't about being perfect, it's about being proactive. Whether you're building an emergency fund, avoiding scams, or cutting costs, every small step adds up to something bigger: peace of mind.

Remember, it's never too late to take control of your finances and protect what you've worked so hard for. Start small, stay consistent, and celebrate every win along the way.

"Smart spending and saving aren't just about money, they're about security, freedom, and living the life you deserve."

Chapter Three

Stretching Retirement Income

"Make Your Money Work as Hard as You Have"

Let me tell you about Marcy. Marcy is one of those people who seems to have figured out the secret to living a full life in retirement. She's in her late 60s, retired from a mid-level management job, and living comfortably enough on her Social Security and a modest pension. But here's what makes Marcy stand out: she didn't settle for just getting by. Marcy wanted to travel, experience new things, and make the most of her retirement.

When we first talked, she told me, "Aaron, I've worked hard my whole life. I don't want to spend my retirement pinching pennies, I want to enjoy it."

Her solution? A little creativity, a lot of planning, and a willingness to hustle. Marcy figured out how to stretch her income by strategically balancing her Social Security, pension, and retirement accounts, and get this, she started a side gig selling handmade crafts at local markets. Between her careful budgeting and that extra income, Marcy didn't just fund her daily expenses, she also paid for three cruises in the last five years.

Marcy's story is proof that with the right strategies, you can make your money work harder for you, even in retirement. Whether you're trying to cover rising costs, support family, or save for a bucket-list adventure, this chapter is all about helping you maximize your income streams so you can live the retirement you've earned.

Maximizing Social Security and VA Benefits

If you're like most retirees, Social Security is a big piece of your income puzzle. Add in VA benefits if you're a veteran, and you've got two reliable streams of income, but how do you make the most of them?

1. Timing Your Social Security Benefits

One of the biggest decisions you'll make in retirement is when to start collecting Social Security. Here's the deal:

- **Start Early (62)**: You'll get smaller monthly payments, but you'll receive them for a longer period.

- **Wait Until Full Retirement Age (66–67)**: You'll get your full benefit.

- **Delay Until 70**: Your monthly payments will increase by about 8% for each year you delay beyond your full retirement age.

Example: Marcy's Social Security Strategy

Marcy decided to delay Social Security until she turned 70. "It wasn't easy," she admitted. "I had to dip into my savings for a few years, but once those bigger checks started coming in, it was worth it." By delaying, Marcy increased her monthly benefit from $1,800 to $2,300, an extra $6,000 a year.

2. VA Benefits for Veterans

As a veteran, you have access to a range of benefits that can supplement your income. Here's what you need to know:

- **VA Disability Compensation**: If you have a service-connected disability, you're entitled to tax-free monthly payments.

- **Aid and Attendance Benefits**: If you need help with daily activities, this benefit can cover caregiving expenses.

- **Pension Programs**: Veterans with limited income may qualify for additional pension support.

Action Step: Check Your Eligibility

If you're not sure what VA benefits you qualify for, visit **VA.gov** or talk to a Veterans Service Officer (VSO). They can guide you through the application process and help you maximize your benefits.

Strategic Withdrawals from Retirement Savings

"Don't Outlive Your Savings"

Managing your retirement accounts is like walking a tightrope: withdraw too much, too quickly, and you could run out of money. But withdraw too little, and you might miss out on enjoying your golden years.

1. Understanding the Rules

- **Required Minimum Distributions (RMDs):** Once you hit age 73 (or 72 if you turned that age before 2023), the IRS requires you to start withdrawing a minimum amount from traditional IRAs and 401(k)s.

- **Tax Implications:** Withdrawals from traditional accounts are taxed as regular income, so it's important to plan for those taxes.

2. The 4% Rule

One popular strategy for retirement withdrawals is the **4% rule**. The idea is to withdraw 4% of your retirement savings in the first year, then adjust for inflation each year after that. This approach helps ensure your money lasts 25–30 years.

Example: Marcy's Withdrawal Strategy

Marcy had $500,000 saved in her 401(k). Using the 4% rule, she withdrew $20,000 in her first year of retirement. Combined with her Social Security and pension, it was enough to cover her expenses while leaving her savings intact for future years.

3. Stagger Withdrawals

If you have multiple accounts (like a 401(k), IRA, and Roth IRA), be strategic about where you pull money from:

- Start with taxable accounts to minimize penalties and taxes.

- Save Roth IRAs for later, as withdrawals are tax-free and don't require RMDs.

Part-Time Work and Side Hustles

Who says retirement means you have to stop working? For some, a part-time job or side hustle isn't just about extra income, it's also a way to stay active, social, and engaged.

1. Low-Stress, Fulfilling Options

Here are a few ideas for part-time work or side gigs that fit into retirement:

- **Consulting or Freelancing:** Use your professional expertise to help businesses or individuals on a flexible schedule.

- **Tutoring or Teaching:** Share your knowledge in subjects you're passionate about. Online platforms like VIPKid or Wyzant make it easy to tutor from home.

- **Crafting or Selling Goods:** Marcy started making handmade candles and selling them at local markets. "I get to be creative, meet new people, and bring in a little extra money," she said.

- **Seasonal Work:** Think tax preparation, retail during the holidays, or helping with tourist attractions in your area.

2. Benefits Beyond the Income

For Marcy, her candle business wasn't just about the money, it gave her a sense of purpose. "It's something I look forward to," she told me. "It keeps me busy and gives me extra cash for things I enjoy, like traveling."

Activity: Create Your Income Strategy

Here's how to map out your retirement income:

1. **List Your Income Sources:** Write down everything, Social Security, VA benefits, pensions, rental income, part-time work, etc.

2. **Estimate Monthly Amounts:** Figure out how much each source contributes.

3. **Plan Withdrawals:** Decide how much to take from retirement accounts each year.

4. **Identify Gaps:** If your income doesn't cover your expenses, consider a part-time job or side hustle.

The Emotional Side of Stretching Your Income

Money isn't just about numbers, it's about freedom. When you're confident in your income strategy, it's easier to relax and focus on enjoying life. Marcy said it best: "For the first time in years, I feel like I'm in control of my money instead of my money controlling me."

Marcy's Breakthrough Moment

After implementing her income strategy, Marcy was able to cover her day-to-day expenses, fund her travel dreams, and even start a savings account for her grandkids. "Retirement doesn't have to feel like a balancing act," she told me. "You just need a plan, and maybe a little creativity."

Action Plan for the Week

Here's what I want you to do this week:

1. **Review Your Benefits:** Check your Social Security statement and VA benefits to make sure you're maximizing what you're entitled to.

2. **Analyze Your Accounts:** Look at your retirement savings and map out a withdrawal strategy.

3. **Explore Side Gigs:** Brainstorm one or two ways to earn extra income that align with your interests.

Making Your Money Work for You

Your retirement income doesn't have to feel limited. With the right strategies, you can stretch your dollars, cover your needs, and fund the experiences that make life worth living.

Start by maximizing your benefits, withdrawing strategically, and exploring ways to bring in extra income. Remember, it's not about working harder, it's about working smarter.

"You've worked hard your whole life. Now, let's make sure your money works just as hard for you."

Part 2:

Building Security & Peace of Mind

Chapter Four

Planning for the Unexpected

"Because Life Doesn't Come with a Script"

Let me let you in on a little secret: I've been that guy. The one on the other end of the line, calling to remind you it's open enrollment, that you're turning 65, or that your Medicare plan is changing. But I wasn't just any consultant, I sold Medicare plans. I was the person helping folks figure out what to do next, how to navigate their options, and how to find the right coverage.

It wasn't an easy job. Honestly, I dreaded those calls sometimes. Selling Medicare plans isn't like selling a car or a product you can touch, it's about trust. And trust isn't something you can build in a quick phone call.

I cared about the work because I believed in it. But I also saw the pitfalls. I saw people confused by the system, pressured into decisions they didn't fully understand, or caught off guard by the fine print. And while there are plenty of good, honest consultants out there, the Medicare world is also full of people looking to take advantage. That's why I'm writing this chapter, to arm you with the knowledge you need to make informed decisions and protect yourself.

The Truth About Medicare Sales

Here's the first thing you need to know: when you're talking to a Medicare consultant, whether it's over the phone or in person, **you do not pay them directly.**

Let me say that louder for the folks in the back: **If someone asks you to pay them, walk away.**

Consultants and brokers are paid commissions by the insurance companies. If a payment is required, it goes directly to the insurance company, not the person helping you. This is how the system is designed, and it's meant to protect you.

But here's the thing: because consultants are paid on commission, some may steer you toward plans that benefit them more than they benefit you. That's why it's so important to stay informed and ask the right questions.

What I Learned as a Medicare Consultant

Selling Medicare plans gave me a front-row seat to the challenges retirees face when it comes to healthcare and insurance. Here are some of the lessons I learned:

1. It's Confusing for a Reason

The Medicare system is complicated, and that complexity can make it easier for bad actors to take advantage of people. Terms like "Part A," "Part B," "Medigap," and "Advantage Plans" can feel like a foreign language.

2. Most People Don't Know Their Rights

One of the most heartbreaking things I saw was how many people didn't realize they had options. They felt pressured to make decisions on the spot or didn't know they could get a second opinion.

3. Trust is Everything

When I was selling plans, my goal was always to help people find what worked best for them, not just what paid the highest commission. But not every consultant works that way. That's why it's critical to know how to spot the good ones from the bad.

How to Navigate Medicare Consultants and Protect Yourself

If you're working with a Medicare consultant or broker, here are some best practices to protect yourself:

1. Verify Their Credentials

Every Medicare consultant should be licensed to sell insurance in your state. Ask for their full name, company, and license number. If they hesitate, that's a red flag.

2. Ask Questions

Don't be afraid to dig into the details. Here are a few questions you should always ask:

- Why are you recommending this plan?

- What are the out-of-pocket costs?

- Will my current doctors and medications be covered?

- Are there any networks or restrictions I should know about?

A good consultant will take the time to explain the answers and make sure you feel confident in your decision.

3. Take Your Time

Medicare has specific enrollment periods, so don't let anyone rush you into making a decision. If a consultant pressures you to act immediately, it's a sign they may not have your best interests at heart.

4. Never Pay the Consultant

As I mentioned earlier, you should never pay a Medicare consultant directly. If someone asks for payment, walk away.

5. Get Everything in Writing

Ask for a written summary of the plan's benefits and costs before you sign anything. This gives you time to review the details and compare your options.

How to Spot and Avoid Medicare Scams

Unfortunately, the Medicare world is full of scams. Here's what to watch out for:

1. Fake Medicare Representatives

Scammers may call claiming to be from Medicare and ask for personal information. Remember: Medicare will never call you unsolicited.

2. High-Pressure Sales Tactics

If someone says, "If you don't act now, you'll lose your coverage," it's a scam. Legitimate consultants won't use scare tactics.

3. Unusual Payment Requests

If someone asks for payment via gift cards, wire transfers, or cryptocurrency, it's 100% a scam.

Action Step: Report scams to 1-800-MEDICARE or your state's insurance department.

Medicare, Medicaid, and VA Benefits: What You Need to Know

1. Medicare

Medicare has gaps in its coverage, and supplemental plans (Medigap) or Medicare Advantage Plans can help fill those gaps.

2. Medicaid

If your income is limited, Medicaid can help cover expenses Medicare doesn't, like long-term care.

3. VA Benefits

If you're a veteran, explore the healthcare options available through the VA. These benefits can complement or even replace Medicare coverage in some cases.

Action Step: Review your healthcare needs and compare them against your current coverage. Use tools like Medicare.gov or consult with a trusted advisor to explore your options.

A Personal Anecdote: The Call I'll Never Forget

I'll never forget one particular call I made as a Medicare consultant. The woman on the other end was sharp as a tack, but she'd been taken advantage of by a so-called "advisor" who convinced her to buy an overpriced plan that didn't even cover her primary doctor. She broke down crying, saying, "I thought I was doing the right thing, but now I feel like I've been cheated."

That call stuck with me because it reminded me why I got into this work in the first place, to help people, not to exploit them. I walked her through her options, found a plan that met her needs, and helped her cancel the overpriced one. By the end of the call, she said, "I wish I'd talked to you first."

Activity: Create Your Consultant Checklist

Here's your checklist for working with a Medicare or insurance consultant:

1. **Verify Credentials:** Name, company, and license number.

2. **Ask Questions:** What are the plan's costs, benefits, and restrictions?

3. **Take Notes:** Write down the details of your conversation.

4. **Request Written Materials:** Get a summary of the plan's benefits.

5. **Avoid Payments:** Never pay a consultant directly.

Protecting Your Peace of Mind

Navigating Medicare and insurance can feel overwhelming, but with the right knowledge, you can make informed decisions and avoid pitfalls. Remember, consultants can be a valuable resource, but the key is knowing how to work with them, and when to walk away.

"Planning for the unexpected isn't about expecting the worst, it's about being ready for the best life has to offer."

Chapter Five

Your Home, Your Sanctuary

"Protect the Place You Call Home"

Let me tell you about my neighbor Mary. Mary and her late husband bought their house over 40 years ago, raised their kids there, and filled it with the kind of memories that stick with you for a lifetime. The dining room table? That's where the kids did their homework. The backyard? That's where the grandkids learned to ride their bikes.

But as Mary got older, the house started feeling less like a sanctuary and more like a challenge. The stairs were harder to climb. The utility bills were creeping up. And the yard, well, let's just say it wasn't going to mow itself.

One day over coffee, Mary looked at me and said, "Aaron, I love this house, but it's not working for me anymore. I don't even know where to start, should I stay, sell, or what?"

Mary's situation isn't unique. For many of us, our homes are more than just a place to live, they're part of who we are. But as we age, our needs change, and sometimes, the home we love doesn't fit our lifestyle anymore. This chapter is all about helping you navigate those tough decisions, protect your property, and find a living arrangement that brings you both comfort and peace of mind.

The Emotional Connection to Your Home

Let's start with the heart of the matter: your home isn't just a building. It's where you've celebrated holidays, raised kids, weathered storms (both literal and figurative), and created memories.

But as much as we love our homes, they can also be a source of stress, especially if they're expensive to maintain or no longer suit your needs. The goal here isn't to tell you what to do. It's to help you weigh your options so you can make the best decision for your future.

Housing Decisions: Stay Put, Downsize, or Move to Senior Living

When it comes to housing in retirement, most people face three main options. Let's break them down with **real-world examples** and explanations.

1. Staying Put

For many people, the idea of leaving their home is unthinkable, and staying put can be a great option if the house still fits your needs.

Pros:

- Familiarity: You know your neighbors, your routines, and where everything is.

- No Moving Costs: Avoid the hassle and expense of selling and moving.

- Emotional Comfort: You stay connected to the memories and milestones tied to your home.

Cons:

- Maintenance: Roofs need repairs, furnaces break down, and the yard doesn't mow itself.
- Accessibility: Stairs, narrow hallways, or outdated bathrooms can become safety issues.
- Expense: Property taxes, utility bills, and upkeep can strain a retirement budget.

Real-World Example:
Mary considered staying put but realized her two-story house wasn't practical anymore. Her bedroom was upstairs, and she found herself avoiding the stairs entirely some days.

Tips for Staying Put:

Make Accessibility Upgrades:

- Install grab bars in the bathroom ($200–$500).

- Add a stairlift (average cost: $3,000–$5,000).

- Replace doorknobs with lever handles ($20–$40 per door).

Create a Maintenance Budget: Set aside money for home repairs and services like lawn care or snow removal.

2. Downsizing

If your home feels like more than you need, downsizing can simplify your life and free up cash for other goals.

- **Pros:**

    - Lower Costs: Smaller homes mean lower utility bills, property taxes, and maintenance expenses.

    - Easier to Manage: Less square footage equals less cleaning and fewer repairs.

    - Financial Freedom: Selling a larger home often gives you a financial cushion for emergencies or travel.

- **Cons:**

    - Emotional Loss: Letting go of a beloved home can be difficult.
    - Moving Expenses: The cost of selling, buying, and moving can add up (average cost: $10,000–$15,000).
    - Adjusting to a New Space: Downsizing means parting with belongings and getting used to a new environment.

Real-World Example:
Mary eventually decided to sell her house and move into a two-bedroom condo. She used the proceeds from the sale to pay off some debts and fund a trip to visit her grandkids.

Tips for Downsizing:

- Start decluttering early, donate, sell, or give away items you don't need.

- Work with a real estate agent who understands the market and can help you price your home competitively.

3. Moving to Senior Living

For some, senior living communities offer the best of both worlds: independence with built-in support.

Types of Senior Living:

- **Independent Living:** For those who don't need daily assistance but want a low-maintenance lifestyle.

- **Assisted Living:** Includes help with daily activities like bathing, dressing, and medication management.

- **Continuing Care Communities:** Offer a range of services, from independent living to skilled nursing, as needs change.

Pros:

- Access to Amenities: Many communities offer meals, transportation, and activities.

- Social Opportunities: Built-in community for making friends and staying active.

- No Maintenance: Say goodbye to home repairs and yard work.

Cons:

- Cost: Monthly fees can range from $2,000 to $6,000 or more, depending on services.

- Adjusting to New Surroundings: Moving to a new environment takes time.

Tips for Choosing Senior Living:

Visit multiple communities to get a feel for the environment.

- Ask about costs, contracts, and what services are included.

- Talk to current residents about their experiences.

Property Insurance: Protecting What Matters

Whether you stay in your home, downsize, or move to a condo, having the right property insurance is essential. Here's what you need to know:

1. What Does Homeowners Insurance Cover?

Homeowners insurance typically includes:

- **Dwelling Coverage:** Repairs for your home after disasters like fire, wind, or hail.

- **Personal Property Coverage:** Replacement for belongings after theft or damage.

- **Liability Coverage:** Protection if someone is injured on your property.

2. Special Considerations for Seniors

- **Riders for High-Value Items:** If you own expensive jewelry, art, or collectibles, consider adding a rider to your policy.

- **Flood or Earthquake Coverage:** These are not typically included in standard policies but may be worth adding, depending on where you live.

3. Insurance for Condos or Rentals

- **Condo Insurance:** Covers the interior of your unit and personal belongings. HOA insurance typically covers the exterior.

- **Renter's Insurance:** If you're renting, this protects your belongings and liability.

Action Step: Review your insurance policy annually to make sure it still meets your needs.

Balancing Sentimental Value with Practicality

Letting go of a home filled with memories is never easy, but here are some ways to preserve those memories while making practical decisions:

1. Create a Memory Box

Take photos of your favorite rooms, record family stories, or keep small mementos that remind you of special moments.

2. Focus on the Future

Think about what a new home or living arrangement could bring, financial freedom, easier maintenance, or new opportunities to connect with others.

3. Involve Your Family

Talk to your kids or grandkids about your plans. They may have insights or be able to help with the transition.

Activity: Housing Decision Worksheet

Here's a simple worksheet to help you decide what's best for you:

1. **What Do You Value Most?**

   - Comfort and familiarity?

   - Financial freedom?

   - Access to support or amenities?

2. **What Are Your Challenges?**

   - Is maintenance becoming a burden?

   - Are accessibility issues affecting your daily life?

   - Do you feel lonely or isolated?

3. **Explore Your Options:**

   - List the pros and cons of staying put, downsizing, or moving to senior living.

4. **Plan Your Next Steps:**

   - If you're staying put, what upgrades or changes are needed?

   - If you're downsizing, what's your timeline for selling and moving?

   - If you're considering senior living, which communities will you visit?

Your Home, Your Future

Your home is your sanctuary, but it's also part of your retirement plan. Whether you choose to stay, sell, or move, the goal is to find a living situation that works for your needs and gives you the freedom to enjoy your retirement.

"Protect your home, preserve your memories, and build a future that feels just right for you."

Chapter Six

Legacy Planning 101

"Because Your Family Deserves Clarity"

Let me tell you about Dave again. You might remember him from earlier in this book. Dave's the kind of guy who always thought he had his ducks in a row. After all, he'd written a will years ago, named his kids as beneficiaries, and even left notes about his final wishes. He figured, "I've done my part, my family's protected."

But when Dave passed away unexpectedly, it turned out things weren't as simple as he thought. His will ended up in probate court, his kids argued over the family home, and a big chunk of his estate went to legal fees. His oldest daughter told me, "I always thought Dad had it all figured out, but this has been a nightmare."

Here's the truth: wills don't protect your assets the way many people believe they do. They're important, but they're only one piece of the puzzle. This chapter is about giving you the real-world tools to ensure your legacy is protected, your family is cared for, and your hard-earned assets go where you want them to go, without unnecessary drama.

The Reality About Wills: What They Do and Don't Do

A will is an essential document, but it has limits. Let's clear up some common misconceptions:

What a Will Does

- **Designates Beneficiaries:** Specifies who gets your property, like your house, savings, or personal belongings.

- **Names an Executor:** Appoints someone to oversee the distribution of your estate.

- **Covers Guardianship:** Allows you to name a guardian for minor children.

What a Will Doesn't Do

- **Avoid Probate:** Many people think a will bypasses probate court, but it doesn't. A will must go through probate, which is a public process that can be expensive and time-consuming.

- **Protect Assets from Creditors:** If you owe money when you pass, creditors can make claims against your estate before your beneficiaries receive anything.

- **Safeguard Against Medicaid Recovery:** If you've used Medicaid for long-term care, the state can seek reimbursement from your estate after you pass.

Pro Tip: A will is a good starting point, but it's not enough to fully protect your family or your assets. That's where trusts, beneficiary designations, and Medicaid planning come in.

Trusts: The Real Power Player in Legacy Planning

Trusts are often misunderstood, but they're one of the most powerful tools for protecting your assets and ensuring your wishes are followed. Unlike a will, a trust doesn't go through probate, offers greater control, and can protect your estate from creditors and Medicaid recovery.

1. Revocable Trusts (Living Trusts)

- **How It Works:** You transfer assets into the trust during your lifetime but maintain control over them. You can change or revoke the trust at any time.

- **Benefits:**

  - Avoids probate, so your assets are distributed faster and privately.

  - Allows you to manage your assets if you become incapacitated.

  - Provides flexibility.

- **Limitations:**

  Doesn't protect assets from creditors or Medicaid recovery.

2. Irrevocable Trusts

- **How It Works:** Once assets are placed in an irrevocable trust, you can't take them back or make changes (with few exceptions).

  Benefits:

- Protects assets from creditors, lawsuits, and Medicaid recovery.

- Can reduce estate taxes for larger estates.

- Ensures your assets are preserved for your beneficiaries.

- **When to Use It:** If you're planning for Medicaid or want to safeguard assets from being spent down for long-term care costs.

Real-World Example:
When Dave's wife decided to update her legacy plan after his passing, I suggested an irrevocable trust. She was worried about Medicaid taking her home if she ever needed nursing care. By transferring the house into the trust, she protected it from Medicaid's five-year look-back period while ensuring it would go to her kids.

Medicaid Asset Protection: Don't Let Long-Term Care Drain Your Legacy

One of the biggest financial risks retirees face is the cost of long-term care. Nursing homes can cost $8,000–$10,000 a month, and Medicare doesn't cover those expenses. Without proper planning, families often have to spend down their assets to qualify for Medicaid.

1. How Medicaid Recovery Works

If Medicaid pays for your long-term care, the state can seek reimbursement from your estate after you pass. This is called Medicaid estate recovery.

2. Protecting Assets with Irrevocable Trusts

Placing assets, like your home or savings, into an irrevocable trust can shield them from Medicaid recovery.

- **Five-Year Look-Back Period:** Medicaid reviews financial transactions from the past five years. Any transfers to a trust must be made outside this window to avoid penalties.

- **What to Include in the Trust:** Your home, savings accounts, or any other assets you want to protect.

Action Step: If you're considering Medicaid planning, start early. Consulting with an elder law attorney can help you navigate the rules and protect your assets.

Key Differences Between Wills and Trusts

Practical Steps for Legacy Planning

Here's a step-by-step guide to get started on protecting your legacy:

1. Start with a Will

- List all your assets, from your home to personal belongings.

- Decide who will inherit what.

- Name an executor and, if applicable, a guardian for

Feature	Will	Trust
Goes Through Probate	Yes	No
Public or Private?	Public	Private
Protects Assets from Creditors	No	Yes (irrevocable trust only)
Controls Distribution Timing	No	Yes
Avoids Medicaid Recovery	No	Yes (irrevocable trust only)

minor children.

2. Consider Adding a Trust

- Use a **revocable trust** to avoid probate and manage assets smoothly.

- Use an **irrevocable trust** to protect assets from creditors and Medicaid.

3. Update Beneficiaries

- Check your life insurance policies, retirement accounts, and bank accounts. Beneficiary designations bypass probate and override wills.

4. Plan for Medicaid Early

- If long-term care is a concern, consult an elder law attorney to explore irrevocable trusts or other Medicaid planning tools.

5. Store Your Documents Safely

- Keep your will, trust, and other important documents in a fireproof safe or with an attorney. Let your executor or a trusted family member know where to find them.

Personal Anecdote: Dave's Wife Gets It Right

After Dave's unexpected passing, his wife, Linda, was determined to avoid the same mistakes. We worked together to create an irrevocable trust for her home and a revocable trust for her savings. She updated her beneficiary designations and wrote a detailed will for her personal belongings.

Six months later, Linda told me, "Aaron, I sleep better at night knowing my kids won't have to guess what I want. They'll have clarity, and that's the greatest gift I can give them."

Activity: Build Your Legacy Plan

Here's a simple checklist to help you get started:

1. **List Your Assets:**

    Home, savings accounts, retirement accounts, personal belongings.

2. **Decide on Beneficiaries:**

    Who will inherit each asset?

3. **Choose Your Tools:**

    Will only.

4. Will + Revocable Trust.

    Will + Irrevocable Trust (if Medicaid planning is needed).

5. **Consult a Professional:**

    Meet with an estate planning attorney or elder law expert to create your documents.

6. **Store and Communicate:**

    Keep everything in a secure location, and make sure your executor knows where to find it.

Protecting Your Family's Future

Legacy planning is about more than dividing assets, it's about giving your family clarity, confidence, and peace of mind. Whether it's creating a will, setting up a trust, or protecting your assets from long-term care costs, the steps you take now will make all the difference later.

"Don't leave your family guessing. Plan today, so tomorrow is clear and calm for the people you love most."

Part 3:

Creating & Celebrating Your Legacy

Chapter Seven

Family Conversations About the Future

"Because Clarity Brings Comfort"

Let me take you back to a Sunday afternoon not long ago. My kids were over for dinner, nothing fancy, just a roast chicken and the usual laughs around the table. But that night, I had something heavier on my mind.

After we finished eating, I cleared my throat and said, "Alright, I need to talk to you all about something important. It's not easy, but it's necessary." You could've heard a pin drop. My kids looked at me like I was about to announce some earth-shattering news.

I told them about my end-of-life wishes. Where I wanted to be buried, what kind of service I'd prefer, and how I planned to divide up my assets. I shared that I'd written everything down in a binder, financial accounts, insurance policies, even the passwords to my digital accounts, and that it was all organized and ready for them when the time came.

My oldest, Nicolas, broke the silence. "Dad, do we really need to talk about this now?"

"Yes," I said. "Because if we don't, you'll be sitting here one day, confused, stressed, and wondering what I would've wanted. And I love you too much to let that happen."

That conversation wasn't easy, but it was one of the most meaningful ones we've ever had. And let me tell you, the relief on their faces when they realized everything was already handled? That made it all worth it.

This chapter is about having those tough but necessary conversations with your loved ones. It's not just about making things easier for them, it's about giving yourself the peace of mind that comes with knowing your wishes will be honored.

Why These Conversations Matter

Talking about the future, your finances, care plans, or even end-of-life wishes, can feel uncomfortable, but here's the truth: avoiding these conversations doesn't make the reality go away. It just leaves your family with unanswered questions, unnecessary stress, and sometimes even conflict.

When you take the time to communicate your plans clearly, you:

- Reduce confusion and stress for your loved ones.

- Prevent family disagreements.

- Ensure your wishes are respected.

How to Start the Conversation

"It's Not Easy, But It's Necessary"

Bringing up these topics can feel daunting. You don't want to upset anyone or make the conversation feel too heavy. Here are some tips for starting the conversation in a way that feels natural and productive:

1. Choose the Right Time and Place

Timing is everything. Pick a moment when everyone is calm and relaxed, maybe over dinner or during a quiet weekend afternoon. Avoid high-stress times, like holidays or immediately after a family disagreement.

2. Start with Your Why

Begin by explaining why you want to have this conversation. For example:

- "I want to make sure you all know my wishes so there's no confusion down the road."

- "It's important to me that we're all on the same page about the future."

3. Keep It Casual at First

You don't need to dive into every detail right away. Start with general topics and ease into the specifics. For example:

- "Have you ever thought about what you'd want if something happened to you?"

- "I've been working on organizing my finances and plans. Can we talk about it so you're aware of what's in place?"

4. Be Reassuring

Let them know this conversation isn't about doom and gloom, it's about being prepared. Say something like:

- "This isn't about expecting the worst, it's about making sure everything is clear and easy when the time comes."

Handling Resistance

"What If They Don't Want to Talk About It?"

It's not uncommon for family members to avoid these conversations. Some people find the topic uncomfortable or overwhelming. Here's how to navigate resistance:

1. Acknowledge Their Feelings

If someone pushes back, validate their emotions. Say something like:

- "I know this isn't an easy topic, but it's important to me that we talk about it."

2. Break It Into Smaller Conversations

You don't have to cover everything in one sitting. If the topic feels too heavy, break it into smaller discussions over time.

3. Share Your Perspective

Explain how planning ahead has helped you feel more at ease. For example:

- "Knowing that everything is organized gives me peace of mind, and I want you to feel that way too."

4. Use Stories to Illustrate

If they're resistant, share a story about someone who didn't plan ahead and the challenges their family faced. Real-world examples can make the need for planning feel more urgent.

Creating a Clear Roadmap

"Because Organization is a Gift to Your Loved Ones"

One of the most helpful things you can do for your family is to create a "legacy binder." This is a single place where all your important information is organized and easily accessible.

What to Include in Your Legacy Binder

1. **Personal Information:**

   - Full name, date of birth, Social Security number.

   - Copies of IDs and health insurance cards.

2. **Financial Information:**

   - Bank account details.

   - Investment accounts and retirement plans.

   - Insurance policies (life, health, property).

3. **Legal Documents:**

   - Will and/or trust documents.

   - Power of attorney.

   - Advance healthcare directive.

4. **Property Information:**

   - Deeds, titles, and mortgage information.

5. **End-of-Life Wishes:**

   - Burial or cremation preferences.

   - Funeral arrangements.

   - Letters to loved ones (if desired).

6. **Digital Information:**

- Passwords for online accounts.

- Instructions for social media accounts.

How to Organize It

- Use a sturdy binder or folder with labeled sections.

- Store it in a fireproof safe or give a copy to a trusted family member.

Personal Anecdote: Why My Binder Brings Me Peace

When I finished putting together my own legacy binder, I felt an unexpected sense of relief. I knew that no matter what happened, my family wouldn't be left guessing about my wishes or scrambling to find important documents.

My son Nicolas, who was initially resistant to having "that talk," told me later, "Dad, I didn't realize how much this would mean to us. Thank you for making it easier."

Activity: Start Your Family Roadmap

Here's a simple exercise to get started:

1. Conversation Starters

Use these prompts to break the ice:

- "If something happened to me, would you know where to find my important documents?"

- "I want to make sure you're not left with any stress or confusion down the road. Can we talk about my plans?"

2. Create Your Binder

- Gather your documents and organize them into categories.

- Use the checklist in this chapter to ensure nothing important is missing.

3. Share with Your Family

- Schedule a time to sit down with your loved ones and walk them through what's in the binder.

Clarity Brings Comfort

Family conversations about the future aren't easy, but they're one of the most loving things you can do for your loved ones. By starting the conversation, addressing resistance, and creating a clear roadmap, you're giving your family the gift of clarity and peace of mind.

"These conversations may be tough, but they're worth it. Because when the time comes, your family will know exactly what you wanted, and that's a comfort money can't buy."

Chapter Eight

Giving Back and Paying It Forward

"Your Legacy Is Bigger Than Dollars and Cents"

Let me tell you about a moment that changed the way I saw retirement. A few years back, I was asked to help out at a local Boys & Girls Club. They needed someone to teach a workshop on basic life skills, stuff like budgeting, job interviews, and even how to change a tire. I figured, *Why not? I've got the time, and maybe I can pass on a little wisdom.*

What I didn't expect was how much *I* would get out of the experience. Seeing those kids light up when they learned something new, or hearing them say, "Wow, no one's ever explained it like that before," reminded me that the most valuable thing we can give isn't money, it's time, knowledge, and care.

That day, I realized something: your legacy isn't just about what you leave behind; it's about what you give while you're here. This chapter is all about finding ways to give back that reflect your values, bring you joy, and make a real impact.

Why Giving Back Matters

Giving back isn't just about helping others, it's about finding purpose and connection. Studies show that volunteering and philanthropy can:

- Boost your mental and emotional well-being.

- Reduce feelings of loneliness or isolation.

- Give you a sense of accomplishment and purpose.

And let's face it, there's no better feeling than knowing you've made a difference in someone else's life.

Volunteering Locally

"Start Close to Home"

Volunteering is one of the most accessible and rewarding ways to give back. The best part? You don't have to look far to find opportunities to make an impact.

1. Finding Opportunities in Your Community

- **Community Centers and Libraries:** These places are often looking for people to help with classes, events, or outreach programs.

- **Food Banks and Shelters:** Many organizations need volunteers to distribute food, serve meals, or organize donations.

- **Schools:** Whether it's tutoring, mentoring, or reading to young children, schools are always grateful for extra hands.

- **Veterans' Organizations:** If you're a veteran, consider giving back through groups like the VFW, American Legion, or VA hospitals.

2. Matching Your Skills to Volunteer Opportunities

Think about what you're good at or passionate about. For example:

- **Good with Finances?** Offer to teach budgeting workshops at a local nonprofit.

- **Love Working with Your Hands?** Help with Habitat for Humanity projects.

- **Enjoy Cooking?** Volunteer to prepare meals at a soup kitchen.

Real-World Example:
After retiring, my friend Pete started volunteering at an animal shelter. He's always been an animal lover, and now he spends his mornings walking dogs and helping with adoptions. "It's the best part of my day," he told me.

Impactful Donations

"It's Not About the Amount, It's About the Impact"

If volunteering isn't your thing, or if you want to give in other ways, financial donations can make a big difference. The key is to make contributions that align with your values and have a meaningful impact.

1. Choosing Where to Donate

- **Start with Your Passions:** What causes are close to your heart? Education, healthcare, the environment?

- **Research Organizations:** Use tools like Charity Navigator or GuideStar to ensure your donations go to reputable nonprofits.

- **Think Local:** Small, local organizations often have a more direct impact on your community.

2. Types of Donations

- **One-Time Gifts:** Perfect for supporting a specific campaign or fundraiser.

- **Recurring Donations:** Monthly contributions provide steady support to organizations you care about.

- **Legacy Gifts:** Include a charitable donation in your will or trust to leave a lasting impact.

Pro Tip: Many nonprofits accept non-cash donations, like stocks, real estate, or even vehicles. These can sometimes offer tax advantages.

Mentoring the Next Generation

"Your Wisdom is Priceless"

One of the most meaningful ways to give back is by mentoring younger people. Whether it's through formal programs or informal relationships, sharing your knowledge and experience can change someone's life.

1. Why Mentoring Matters

Young people, whether they're teenagers, college students, or young professionals, often benefit from guidance and encouragement. As a mentor, you can:

- Help them navigate challenges and make informed decisions.

- Share lessons you've learned from your own successes and mistakes.

- Be a positive role model and a source of support.

2. How to Get Started

- **Join a Mentorship Program:** Look for programs through local schools, community centers, or professional organizations.

- **Be Open to Informal Mentoring:** Sometimes, it's as simple as offering advice to a neighbor's kid or sharing career tips with a young coworker.

- **Use Online Platforms:** Websites like SCORE (for small business mentoring) or Big Brothers Big Sisters often have opportunities to mentor remotely.

Real-World Example:
A retired teacher I know started mentoring college students through her alumni association. She told me, "It's so rewarding to help these kids figure out their paths, and it keeps me feeling sharp, too."

Creating a "Giving Back Plan"

"Align Your Skills and Values with Your Actions"

Here's how to create a personalized plan for giving back:

1. Reflect on Your Values

Ask yourself:

- What causes or issues are most important to me?

- What skills or experiences can I share with others?

2. Set Goals

Decide what kind of impact you want to make. For example:

- Volunteering 10 hours a month.

- Donating a set percentage of your income.

- Mentoring one young person each year.

3. Take Action

- Research organizations or programs that align with your goals.

- Schedule your volunteer time or set up recurring donations.

- Reach out to local groups to see where your skills are needed.

Personal Anecdote: How Giving Back Changed Me

That workshop at the Boys & Girls Club wasn't just a way to give back, it gave me a sense of purpose I didn't even know I needed. Retirement can feel a little aimless sometimes, but finding ways to contribute reminded me that I still have so much to offer.

Whether it's sharing your time, your resources, or your wisdom, giving back isn't just about others, it's about enriching your own life, too.

Activity: Build Your Giving Back Plan

Here's a simple exercise to get you started:

1. **List Your Skills and Interests:**

   - What are you good at?

   - What do you enjoy doing?

2. **Identify Causes You Care About:**

   - Education, healthcare, the environment, veterans, animal welfare, etc.

3. **Research Opportunities:**

   - Look for local organizations or programs that align with your interests.

4. **Set a Goal:**

   - How much time, money, or energy do you want to commit?

5. **Take the First Step:**

   - Make a call, send an email, or sign up for a volunteer event this week.

A Legacy of Impact

Your legacy isn't just about what you leave behind, it's about how you live and what you give while you're here. Whether it's volunteering, donating, or mentoring, giving back is one of the most meaningful ways to make a difference.

"The greatest legacy isn't money, it's the love, wisdom, and kindness you share with the world."

Chapter Nine

Your Final Chapter, Written Your Way

"Leave the Legacy You Want"

Let me tell you about my friend Charlie. Charlie was one of the most thoughtful and intentional people I've ever known. He didn't just live life, he planned for it, every step of the way. And when the time came for us to say goodbye to Charlie, I realized that even in his absence, he'd managed to bring us all together in a way that felt uniquely him.

Charlie's memorial wasn't just a service, it was a celebration. There were photos from his adventures, stories from friends, and even a playlist of his favorite songs. His kids read letters he'd written to them, and his grandkids shared how much they'd learned from him. By the end, there wasn't a dry eye in the room, but there were also smiles and laughter.

That day, I realized something important: your legacy isn't just about what you leave behind, it's about how you make people feel when you're gone. Charlie had planned his final chapter with the same care he lived his life, and it left an impact none of us will ever forget.

This chapter is about helping you write your own final chapter, your way. Whether it's planning your memorial, creating meaningful keepsakes, or sharing wisdom with your loved ones, this is your chance to leave a legacy that truly reflects who you are.

Planning Funerals and Memorials

"Because Your Final Wishes Should Be Respected"

One of the best ways to take the burden off your family is to plan your funeral or memorial in advance. It might feel uncomfortable to think about, but it's a gift of clarity and comfort for your loved ones.

1. Decide What Matters Most to You

Ask yourself:

- Do I want a funeral, memorial service, or celebration of life?

- Where would I like it to take place (a church, a park, or somewhere special to me)?

- What kind of tone do I want, formal, casual, celebratory?

2. Document Your Wishes

Put your preferences in writing so your family knows exactly what you want. Be specific about:

- Burial or cremation preferences.

- Type of service (religious, non-religious, etc.).

- Music, readings, or speakers you'd like included.

3. Consider Pre-Planning

Many funeral homes offer pre-planning services, which allow you to make arrangements and pay in advance. This can save your family from financial stress and decision-making during a difficult time.

Pro Tip: Keep a copy of your funeral preferences in your legacy binder and share them with a trusted family member.

Creating Meaningful Memories

"Because Your Story Deserves to Be Told"

Your legacy isn't just about the event of your passing, it's about the memories, stories, and wisdom you leave behind for your loved ones.

1. Write Legacy Letters

A legacy letter is a personal note to someone you care about. It can include:

- Words of encouragement or advice.

- Stories or memories you want them to remember.

- Expressions of love or gratitude.

You can write one for each of your children, grandchildren, or even close friends.

2. Create Photo Albums or Scrapbooks

Collect photos, mementos, and captions that tell the story of your life. This can become a treasured keepsake for your family.

3. Record Messages

Leave behind video or audio messages for your loved ones. Whether it's sharing a favorite memory or offering advice, these recordings can become priceless reminders of your voice and personality.

Example:

My friend Donna recorded a video for her grandkids, sharing stories about her childhood and what she hoped for their futures. "I wanted them to know who I was, not just as their grandmother, but as a person," she told me.

Beyond Money: Leaving a Legacy of Love, Kindness, and Wisdom

"The Greatest Gifts Can't Be Measured in Dollars"

While financial planning is an important part of your legacy, the most impactful legacies go beyond money. They're about the love, values, and lessons you pass down.

1. Share Your Wisdom

Think about the life lessons you've learned and how you can share them with your family. For example:

- Write down your "golden rules" for living.

- Share your thoughts on resilience, kindness, or gratitude.

2. Be a Role Model

Your actions in life, how you treat others, the causes you support, and the way you face challenges, leave an impression that lasts long after you're gone.

3. Strengthen Relationships

Don't wait for the "right time" to tell people how much they mean to you. Express your love, apologize if needed, and create memories now that will live on.

Personal Anecdote: How Charlie's Legacy Taught Me What Matters

At Charlie's memorial, his son stood up and said, "My dad didn't leave me a fortune, but he left me something even better, a lifetime of lessons about how to be a good person." That stuck with me because it reminded me that our real legacy isn't in our bank accounts, it's in the lives we touch.

Activity: Plan Your Legacy

Here's an exercise to help you get started:

1. Reflect on Your Legacy

Ask yourself:

- What do I want people to remember about me?

- What values or lessons do I want to pass on?

2. Write a Legacy Letter

Pick one person you care about and write them a letter. Share a memory, a piece of advice, or a heartfelt message of love.

3. Outline Your Memorial Preferences

Use this template to document your wishes:

- **Service Type:** Funeral, memorial, or celebration of life?

- **Location:** Church, park, home, or other?

- **Tone:** Formal, casual, celebratory?

- **Music or Readings:** Specific songs, poems, or scriptures you want included?

- **Speakers:** Who would you like to share memories or speak at your service?

4. Create a Keepsake

Decide how you'd like to share your story, whether it's a photo album, video recording, or scrapbook.

Write Your Final Chapter Your Way

Planning your final chapter isn't about focusing on the end, it's about creating something that reflects the life you've lived and the legacy you want to leave behind.

When you take the time to plan your memorial, create keepsakes, and share your wisdom, you're giving your loved ones the ultimate gift: clarity, comfort, and a lasting connection to the person you are.

"Your final chapter is yours to write, make it one that inspires, uplifts, and leaves the world a little brighter for having known you."

Chapter Ten

Resources and Research

"The Evidence Behind the Advice"

This chapter serves as a guide to the research, tools, and trusted resources that inspired the strategies and insights shared throughout this book. Whether you're interested in understanding the studies behind the advice, accessing additional tools, or exploring more on specific topics, this section is your go-to. It's designed to help you take control of your finances, health, and legacy with confidence and clarity.

Highlighted Research and Studies

Here are some key studies, data points, and authoritative sources referenced in this book:

Social Security Optimization

Stat: Delaying Social Security beyond full retirement age increases your benefits by approximately 8% per year until age 70.

> **Source:** Social Security Administration (SSA) , www.ssa.gov

The 4% Rule for Retirement Savings

Stat: The 4% withdrawal rule is a guideline that suggests withdrawing 4% of your retirement savings in the first year and adjusting for inflation thereafter. This approach helps ensure that savings last 25–30 years.

> **Source:** William Bengen, "Determining Withdrawal Rates Using Historical Data" (1994).

VA Benefits for Veterans

Stat: Eligible veterans can access Aid and Attendance benefits to help cover caregiving expenses or additional support for daily activities.

> **Source:** U.S. Department of Veterans Affairs , www.va.gov

Mental and Physical Health Benefits of Social Connection

Stat: Research shows that strong social ties can lower the risk of depression, improve cardiovascular health, and extend life expectancy.

> **Source:** Mayo Clinic , "The Role of Social Support in Healthy Aging" (2020).

Trusted Resources

Below are some of the most reliable organizations and tools to support your journey:

Financial Planning and Retirement Tools

- **My Social Security:** Create an account to view your earnings history, estimate benefits, and manage your Social Security.
  www.ssa.gov/myaccount

- **AARP Retirement Calculator:** A simple tool to help you estimate income, expenses, and savings goals for retirement.
  www.aarp.org/retirement

- **Personal Capital:** An app to track your spending, savings, and investments.
  www.personalcapital.com

Veteran-Specific Resources

- **Veterans Service Officers (VSOs):** Connect with a VSO for free assistance in applying for VA benefits.
  www.va.gov/vso

- **Veterans Crisis Line:** Support for veterans in crisis or dealing with mental health challenges.
  Dial 988, then press 1 or visit www.veteranscrisisline.net.

Health and Wellness Tools

- **Mayo Clinic Healthy Aging Program:** Resources on nutrition, fitness, and maintaining physical health as you age.
  www.mayoclinic.org/healthy-aging

- **SilverSneakers:** A fitness program offering free or discounted access to gyms and classes for seniors.
  www.silversneakers.com

Estate and Legacy Planning Tools

- **LegalZoom:** Affordable solutions for creating wills, trusts, and other legal documents.
  www.legalzoom.com

- **Everplans:** A digital tool to organize your estate planning documents, account details, and personal wishes in one secure place.
  www.everplans.com

Practical Tools and Worksheets

Here are some simple tools to help you take action:

1. **Budget Worksheet:** A downloadable or printable worksheet to track monthly income and expenses.
   Example categories include housing, healthcare, travel, and discretionary spending.

2. **Legacy Binder Checklist:** Use this to organize critical documents like wills, financial accounts, insurance policies, and personal letters.

- Include: Account passwords, contact lists, and instructions for loved ones.

3. **Exercise Tracker:** A simple log for tracking daily movement, stretching, and fitness goals.

FAQs and Common Questions

What is the best age to start collecting Social Security?

The best age depends on your personal circumstances. If you can delay until age 70, you'll receive the maximum benefit. However, if you need income earlier, starting at full retirement age (66–67) ensures you receive your full primary insurance amount.

How do I apply for VA benefits?

Visit www.va.gov to explore benefits and start an application. For personalized help, contact a Veterans Service Officer (VSO).

What is the 4% withdrawal rule?

It's a guideline for managing retirement savings: withdraw 4% of your savings in the first year, then adjust for inflation each year. This approach balances your income needs with the goal of preserving your savings.

Closing Note

Thank you for taking the time to engage with this section. The resources, tools, and research shared here are meant to empower you to take full control of your retirement and legacy planning. Remember, your financial security and personal legacy are well within your reach, one thoughtful step at a time.

Let's make your hard work count for the years ahead.

Securing Your Future, Protecting Your Family
"Because the Best Legacies Start with Thoughtful Planning"

Let me start by saying this: if you've made it to the end of this book, you're already ahead of the game. Taking the time to think about your future, your finances, and your family is no small thing, it's a powerful act of love and responsibility.

Throughout these chapters, we've talked about the practicalities of budgeting, safeguarding your home, planning for unexpected events, and crafting a legacy that reflects your values. We've explored ways to stretch your income, give back to your community, and have those all-important conversations with your loved ones. Every topic ties back to one simple truth: thoughtful preparation brings peace of mind, not just for you, but for everyone who cares about you.

Why This Matters

Here's the thing about planning: it's not just about numbers on a spreadsheet or documents in a binder. It's about the bigger picture, protecting the life you've built, caring for the people you love, and ensuring your legacy reflects the person you are.

When you take the time to plan:

- **You Reduce Stress for Your Family.** By organizing your finances and documenting your wishes, you spare your loved ones from unnecessary confusion and conflict.

- **You Gain Confidence in Your Future.** Knowing your finances and plans are in order lets you focus on living fully and enjoying the time you have.

- **You Leave a Legacy of Love and Clarity.** The best gift you can give your family is the peace of mind that comes from knowing exactly what you wanted.

How Both Books Work Together

This book, *"Legacy Secured: Protect Your Finances, Family, and Future,"* is the perfect companion to its predecessor, *"Thrive After 70: The Veteran's Guide to Living Fully and Aging Gracefully."* While *Thrive After 70* focuses on living with purpose, building meaningful relationships, and enjoying your golden years, *Legacy Secured* dives deeper into the practical side of protecting what you've built.

Together, these books provide a comprehensive roadmap for living fully while planning wisely. They work hand in hand to help you balance the joys of the present with the responsibilities of securing the future, for yourself and for the people you care about. Whether you're exploring ways to rediscover purpose in retirement or ensuring your legacy is protected, these books are here to guide you every step of the way.

Explore My Other Works

If you've found value in this book, you might also enjoy some of my other works, which focus on practical life skills, financial literacy, and personal growth. Books like *"Budget Like a Boss"* and *"Money Adventure"* are designed to help readers of all ages take control of their finances, while *"The Entrepreneur's Playbook"* and *"Strategic Empathy"* offer tools for leadership and success in the workplace.

Each of my books is written with the same goal in mind: to make life's toughest topics more accessible, actionable, and empowering. Whether you're starting fresh, growing your career, or guiding the next generation, these resources are designed to meet you where you are and help you move forward with confidence.

Introducing BuildingBlocs

Another resource I'm proud to share is **BuildingBlocs**. This platform is designed to provide adults, seniors, and even their grandchildren with the tools they need to thrive in today's world.

For adults, BuildingBlocs offers programs on financial literacy, personal growth, and legacy planning, all the skills you need to navigate life's challenges with clarity and confidence. And for grandparents who want to support their grandchildren, it's a way to share practical life skills and create meaningful intergenerational connections.

The goal of Building Blocs is simple: to empower families to learn, grow, and succeed together. Whether it's through workshops, books, or online resources, this platform is a hub for education and inspiration at every stage of life.

To learn more, visit www.buildingblocs.org and explore how you and your family can benefit from these life-changing programs.

Reflecting on Your Journey

As we close this book, I encourage you to take a moment to reflect on your journey. Think about the steps you've already taken and the ones you're ready to take next.

Ask yourself:

1. **What Have I Accomplished?**

   - Have I created a budget that works for my retirement?

   - Have I protected my home and assets?

   - Have I started conversations with my family about the future?

2. **What's Next?**

   - Do I need to set up a trust or finalize my will?

- Are there areas where I can give back or share my wisdom?

- What steps can I take this week to move forward?

A Roadmap for Moving Forward

If you're feeling overwhelmed or unsure of where to start, don't worry, you don't have to do everything at once. Planning is a process, and every small step you take brings you closer to your goals.

Here's a simple roadmap to guide you:

1. **Start with What Matters Most:** Whether it's organizing your finances, protecting your home, or writing a legacy letter, choose one area to focus on first.

2. **Get the Right Help:** Work with professionals like financial advisors, estate planners, or elder law attorneys to ensure your plans are legally sound and effective.

3. **Share Your Plans:** Talk to your family about what you've put in place and how they can access important documents when the time comes.

4. **Review and Revise as Needed:** Life changes, and so should your plans. Make it a habit to review your finances and legacy documents every few years.

The Gift of Peace of Mind

When I think back to the stories I've shared in this book, about my friend Dave, my neighbor Mary, or even my own family, it's clear to me that the most powerful legacy we can leave isn't just financial security. It's peace of mind. It's knowing that your loved ones will have clarity, comfort, and confidence in the plans you've made for them.

Planning doesn't erase life's uncertainties, but it gives you and your family the tools to face them with strength and grace.

A Final Word from Uncle Aaron

Before we wrap up, let me leave you with this: planning for the future isn't just about getting your affairs in order, it's about honoring the life you've lived and ensuring your values carry on. It's about protecting what matters most: your family, your home, and the legacy you leave behind.

You've already taken the most important step by committing to this journey. Now, it's time to keep moving forward. Take what you've learned, put it into action, and trust that every small step you take is making a difference, not just for you, but for the people you love most.

"Your legacy isn't just about what you leave behind, it's about how you live today. So live fully, plan thoughtfully, and leave the world a little brighter for having known you."

Call to Action: Take the Next Step

Here's your final homework assignment:

1. **Choose One Actionable Step:** Pick one thing from this book that resonated with you and commit to completing it this week.

2. **Share Your Plans:** Talk to at least one family member about what you've learned and how you're planning for the future.

3. **Visit BuildingBlocs:** Explore www.buildingblocs.org to discover programs and tools that can help you and your family continue learning and growing together.

4. **Celebrate Your Progress:** Recognize the effort you've made to protect your future and your family, it's no small thing.

Thank You for Reading

Thank you for allowing me to be part of your journey. Writing this book has been an honor, and my hope is that it leaves you feeling empowered, inspired, and ready to take on the next chapter of your life.

With gratitude,
Uncle Aaron